THE RIGHT TO SMOKE?

EMMA HAUGHTON

SEA-TO-SEA

Mankato Collingwood London

This edition first published in 2006 by
Sea-to-Sea Publications
1980 Lookout Drive
North Mankato
Minnesota 56003

Copyright © Sea-to-Sea Publications 2006

Printed in China

Library of Congress Cataloging-in-Publication Data

Haughton, Emma.
  The right to smoke? / by Emma Haughton.
    p. cm. — (Viewpoints)
  Originally published: New York: Franklin Watts, 1997.
  Includes bibliographical references and index.
  ISBN 1-932889-62-0
    1. Tobacco habit—Juvenile literature. 2. Cigarette habit—Juvenile literature. 3.
Smoking—Juvenile literature. I. Title. II. Viewpoints (Franklin Watts, inc.)

HV5733.H36 2005
362.29'6—dc22

2004062523

9 8 7 6 5 4 3 2

Published by arrangement with the Watts Publishing Group Ltd, London

Photographic credits:
b=bottom; t=top; r=right; l=left
Mary Evans Picture Library: 4b, 10b, 28b;
Eye Ubiquitous: 12b;
Format: Melanie Friend 18t,
Brenda Prince 14b;
David Hoffman 28t;
Hulton Picture Library 11t;
Hutchison Library: Robin Constable 10t, Philip Wolmuth 15b,
Melanie Friend 29b;
Martin Breese/Retrograph Archive8t;
No Smoking Day 26t;
Robert Opie 6;
Popperfoto 8b, 23b, 25bl;
Rex Features, 5t, 9(both), 11b, 12t, 14t, 17t,
  19t, 21t, 24, 25br, 29t, John Downing 16;
Steve Shott cover, 1, 13(both), p.17b, 21b;
Frank Spooner Pictures: Paul Nightingale 22;
Science Photo Library: A Glauberman 7b, Custom Medical
Stock Photo 15t,
Biophoto Associates 25tl,
PA Photos/Peter Jordan 20;
Sygma 7t;
Topham Picture Source, 4t, 19b, 23t,
Press Association/Topham, 27;
Trip: K. Cardwell 5b,
H. Rogers 18b,
A. Kuznetsov 25tr.

Quotation credits, given from the top of a page beginning with the left-
hand column:
p.5 1 Professor Michael Russell, head of the Addiction Research Unit,
Institute of Psychiatry, London; 2 Patrick Reynolds, from his speech posted
at www.saferchild.org/tobacco.htm, 19:9:03
p.6 King James I of England and VI of Scotland, 1603
p.7 1 UK Health Eductaion Authority, 1991; 2 Tom Carter

p.8 Bryan Appleyard, *Independent*, March 8, 1995
p.9 1 David Simpson, director, International Agency on Tobacco and
Health; 2 Richard Klein, *Cigarettes are Sublime*
p.10 1 Professor Michael Russell, source as p.5 1; 2 Lisa;
3 Oscar Wilde, 1891
p.12 Americans for Non-Smokers Rights
p.13 1 Jonathan; 2 Bryan Appleyard, *Independent*, March 8, 1995; 3 Dr.
Matin Jarvis, head of the Imperial Cancer Research Fund's (ICRF) health
behavior unit
p.14 Joanna Smith, mother
p.15 U.S. Environmental Protection Agency (EPA); 2 Americans for Non-
Smokers Rights; 3 Richard Klein, *Guardian*, May 29, 1995
p.16 1 UK Health Education Authority; 2 Dr. Judith Mackay, adivser on
smoking to Asian governments and health
promotion agencies
p.17 Chris Rissel, Clinical Senoir Lecturer, University of Sydney, from his
speech posted at www.pha.org.au, 19:9:03
p.18 Tobacco Advisory Council
p.19 1 Paul Thomas, newsagent, Brighton, UK; 2 Amanda Sandford,
information manager, Action on Smoking and Health (ASH)
p.20 Richard Klein, *Guardian*, May 29, 1995
p.21 1 Professor Michael Russell, source as p.5 1; 2 Tobacco Advisory
Council
p.22 1 Tobacco Manufacturers' Association; 2 Amanda Sandford, source
as p.19 2; 3 Professor Michael Russell source as p. 5 1
p.23 Freedom Organization for the Right to Enjoy Smoking (FOREST), UK
p.24 1 Tobacco Advisory Council on government tobacco duty; 2 Martin
Jarvis, ICRF, *Independent*, July 31, 1995
p.26 1 Frank Woeckel, originally quoted in *Bild* newspaper www.bild-
online.de, 19:9:03; 2 Marjorie Nicholson, spokesperson for FOREST,
August 10, 1995
p.27 1 Dr. David Kessler, former head of the Food and Drug
Administration; 2 UK Department of Health www.doh.gov.uk, 19:9:03
p.28 1 Dr. Martin Jarvis, source as p.13 3; 2 Scott Ballin, head lobbyist for
the U.S. Coalition on Smoking OR Health
p.29 Arnold Trebech, former director, U.S. Drug Policy Foundation

Contents

Who smokes?

Humans have smoked tobacco for a long time. There is evidence of smoking in the Maya civilization of Central America, where tobacco originated, as long ago as A.D. 500. It was brought to Europe by the explorers of the 16th century—Sir Walter Raleigh, for example, organized a massive tobacco shipment to England from the West Indies.

However, it was the invention of a machine to manufacture cigarettes at the end of the 19th century that made smoking so widespread in the 20th. Cigarette consumption rose steadily to 1945, when it also became more common for women to smoke. But from the mid-1970s smoking began to decline in many Western countries; in the USA, for example, about a third of men smoke now compared with about two thirds in 1945.

Around the world roughly one-

▲ *Earlier this century smoking was seen as a stylish activity, especially among women. As you can see, cigarette holders were all the rage.*

▼ *Sir Walter Raleigh introduced tobacco to England in the 16th century. Some people found the new custom a little unnerving!*

third of adults puff their way through 5.5 trillion (5,500,000,000,000) cigarettes a year. Over 46.5 million in the United States (that's 17 percent of the population) smoke, almost equally split between men and women.

While smoking is falling in most Western countries, it is rapidly increasing in Africa, Latin America, and Asia. China alone has more than 300 million smokers. Asia generally is experiencing a smoking epidemic; almost two-thirds of men smoke, with more starting every day. Although currently only 4 percent of Asian women smoke, that figure is predicted to grow rapidly. This is encouraged by the tobacco companies, who are always on the look out for new markets—British

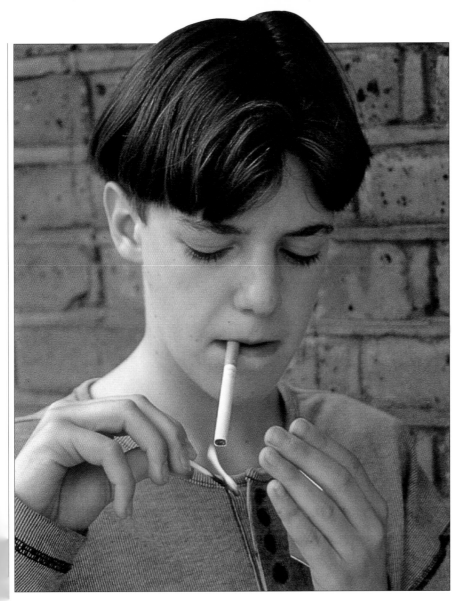

one million more teenagers picking up the habit every year.

Most smokers start young—some are just three years old when they try their first cigarette. In the USA, 90 percent of adult smokers began before they were 18 years old, with 14 the average starting age. For the tobacco industry these young smokers are customers that will generate future profits.

❝ *How long does it take to get hooked? A September 2000 study shows that one-quarter of 12- to 13-year-olds who smoke as few as one or two cigarettes a day become addicted in just two weeks.* **❞**
Patrick Reynolds, antismoking campaigner

▼ *Although cigarettes are becoming less popular in rich Western countries, more people are starting to smoke in other parts of the world. In Asia, for instance, almost two-thirds of men now smoke.*

▲ *Studies show that teenage smoking is on the increase, despite government efforts to bring it down. Most smokers begin as teenagers.*

American Tobacco, for instance, began targeting East European countries after the breakup of the Soviet Union.

Smoking rates tend to be highest among the poor. In the UK, for example, unskilled working men are three times more likely to smoke than professional men. Some of the highest smoking rates are found among the unemployed.

❝ *There's a huge social divide surrounding smoking. The people really killed by smoking are the poor and underprivileged who can't afford things like nicotine replacement treatment to help them give up.* **❞**
Professor Michael Russell, head of the Addiction Research Unit, Institute of Psychiatry, London

Smoking is also related to age. While smokers aged 35-49 consume the most cigarettes, it is teenage smoking that is causing most concern. In the US more than three million teenagers smoke, with about

Slow-motion suicide?

When Europeans started smoking tobacco in pipes in the 16th century, they were not aware of the risks to their health.

However, some, like King James I of England and VI of Scotland, took an educated guess.

❝*A custom loathsome to the eye, hateful to the nose, harmful to the brain, dangerous to the lungs, and in the black stinking fume thereof, nearest resembling the horrible Stigian smoke of the pit that is bottomless...* ❞ *King James I of England and VI of Scotland, 1603*

It was not until the 1950s, when cigarettes had become very popular, that doctors began to research links between smoking and lung disease. They did not prove smoking was a cause of lung cancer and chronic bronchitis until 1962, or a major cause of coronary heart disease until the 1970s.

Today the effects of smoking are well known. In each cigarette a powerful drug called nicotine makes the heart beat faster while narrowing the blood vessels and raising blood pressure. Carbon monoxide, also one of the main gases in exhaust fumes, is produced as tobacco burns, starving the heart of oxygen. Sticky tar from the smoke collects in the lungs. Tobacco smoke contains more than 4,000 chemicals, many of them harmful. Just one drop of pure nicotine on your tongue

Craven 'A'
FOR YOUR THROAT'S SAKE

◀ *Cigarettes were not always believed to be a health risk. This brand even boasted that it was "good for your throat"; smoking is now identified as a cause of throat cancer.*

At 120 years old, Jeanne Louise Calment, became the oldest known person in 1995. She gave up smoking aged 117, only to start again when she was 118! She lived to be 122.

would kill you. Other poisons include hydrogen cyanide (used in some U.S. states to adminster the death penalty), arsenic, benzene, formaldehyde, radioactive compounds, pesticides and toxic metals.

Smoking causes 90 percent of lung cancer, bronchitis, and emphysema deaths, and 25 percent of coronary heart-disease deaths. It is linked with cancers of the mouth, throat, esophagus, bladder, pancreas, kidneys, and cervix, and accounts for one-third of cancer deaths. Smoking also causes breathlessness, persistent coughs, discolored teeth and fingers, bad breath, and premature wrinkling. However, recent evidence suggests that nicotine may reduce the risk of developing brain disorders like Alzheimer's, Parkinson's and motor neuron disease.

Joe Califano, U.S. Secretary for Health in the 1980s, described smoking as "slow-motion suicide." The statistics support him.

**" ***Worldwide it is estimated that by the 2020s, if there is no change in current levels of tobacco consumption, there will be ten million deaths from smoking a year.* **" ***UK Health Education Authority (HEA)*

The lung on the right belonged to a smoker. Compare it to the nonsmoker's lung beside it and you can see the damage done by cigarettes.

Every year in the United States, around 430,700 people die from smoking-related diseases. It has been found that, on average, smokers lose 10 to 15 years from their lives, with almost half dying before retirement.

Although people are aware of these risks, it does not always stop them from smoking.

" ***I've been smoking for thirty years and I've hardly had a day off sick. A lot of this health stuff is out to scare you, but if it's true, so what? We've all got to die of something.* **"
Tom Carter, 68

Even tobacco chiefs are not immune. In 1994, R.J. Reynolds, grandson of the U.S. tobacco company founder, was the fifth Reynolds to die of smoking-related causes.

Why start smoking?

Smoking has long been seen as glamorous. In previous centuries cigars and pipes were common items for rich gentlemen; as cigarettes became popular in the 20th century, it gradually became fashionable for both men and women to smoke. Watch any old black-and-white movie, and you will probably see many people smoking.

66 Casablanca *without cigarettes is unthinkable;* Casablanca *without cigarettes would be a fascist movie. Plus in every modern war the smoking soldier has been an icon of noble endurance...* 99
Bryan Appleyard, journalist

Today most Western people are aware of the dangers of cigarettes, and many smokers are trying to quit. In other, poorer, parts of the world, however, cigarettes are associated with more glamorous and wealthy lifestyles—images deliberately fostered by the tobacco companies.

CIGARETTES PRIMEROSE
BOUT PÉTALE DE ROSE
RÉGIE FRANÇAISE

▲ Advertisers have promoted smoking as stylish and elegant for many years, as shown in this 1920s French advertisement.

Even today, despite all we know about smoking and its dangers, cigarettes still hold an irresistible appeal for many, particularly the young. Smoking is often associated with rock stars, actors, or other celebrities—another association subtly

◀ Humphrey Bogart, **Casablanca**'s star, was rarely seen without a cigarette—it was part of his "tough-guy" image. But smoking brought about Bogart's death of lung cancer at the age of 57.

▲ *The first cigarette, like the first alcoholic drink, is often seen as a beginning of adulthood. You are also much more likely to try a cigarette after a drink, as alcohol lowers your inhibitions.*

promoted by tobacco companies who know that most smokers get hooked in their teens.

Most people hate the taste and sensations of their first cigarette—it is common to feel dizzy or even sick—yet many try again. Why? For young people who live with parents or other relatives who smoke, cigarettes may seem a normal part of growing up. Some teenagers take up smoking because they think it looks cool, sophisticated, or they want to fit in with their friends. For others, it is simply curiosity or a desire to show off. Like trying your first alcoholic drink, smoking is often seen as an introduction to the adult world. Teenagers take up smoking in the belief it makes them look mature; sadly, for most people, it usually suggests the opposite.

After all, is it really glamorous to do something that involves so many health risks? For many the answer is obvious.

66 *For a cosmetics firm to have a model who smokes is a bit like leaving a Rolls-Royce showroom in the hands of a sandpaper salesman.* **99** *David Simpson, director, International Agency on Tobacco and Health, about a leading cosmetic company's choice of model*

Many smokers, however, simply argue that it is a habit they enjoy. Richard Klein, author of *Cigarettes are Sublime*, believes that cigarettes give people a lot of pleasure, and that this is the main reason they choose to smoke.

66 *Tobacco, like alcohol, is a substance in universal use, and must be presumed to have benefits for human civilization if it has been consumed so avidly for so long.* **99** *Richard Klein, Cigarettes are Sublime*

But it is a fact that most people who start smoking wish they had not and most want to kick the habit. What begins as a dare or a desire to be accepted can quickly turn into an addiction. And once you are addicted, it can become very difficult to stop.

▼ *For many, smoking continues to have a cool and sophisticated image, despite the health risks. Smoking in movies and on TV often reinforces this. Here, the actress Uma Thurman smokes in one of the hit movies of the 1990:* **Pulp Fiction.**

Gasping for a cigarette?

Nicotine, a powerful drug present naturally in tobacco, is highly addictive. When people smoke, nicotine reaches the brain via the lungs in seconds, making them feel more relaxed if they are tense, or more alert and active if they are feeling tired.

Teenagers can become addicted to nicotine very rapidly.

Young people only need to smoke a few cigarettes to have over a 90 percent chance of becoming a dependent smoker as an adult. You quickly become tolerant to the unpleasant side effects, especially if social pressure makes you keep going. Professor Michael Russell, head of the Addiction Research Unit, Institute of Psychiatry, London

Although smokers find cigarettes pleasurable, it is not just down to nicotine. Many people find the act of smoking itself comforting in times of stress, or they simply enjoy the ritual of lighting up over a cup of coffee or after a meal.

Some people, however, see themselves purely as social smokers, having only the occasional cigarette. They deny that they are addicted.

I sometimes have a cigarette when I'm out, especially if I'm with other smokers. I don't need one the rest of the time. Lisa, 30

▲ Relaxing with coffee and cigarettes is a pleasure many people enjoy. However, one sign of addiction in a smoker is that he or she finds it impossible to relax without a cigarette.

Unfortunately most smokers want to follow one cigarette with another—and another, sometimes only minutes after the last.

A cigarette is the perfect type of the perfect pleasure. It is exquisite, and it leaves one unsatisfied. What more can one want? Oscar Wilde, 1891

Wilde knew that the effects of nicotine do not last, and as the pleasure wears off, the craving for another cigarette begins. This cycle of addiction leads people to "chain-

◀ The famous playwright and renowned wit, Oscar Wilde, understood very well the cycle of addiction that leaves smokers craving another cigarette soon after they have finished their last.

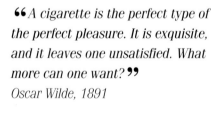

▲ *"Smokers Anonymous" was formed to help smokers to quit in 1956. Meetings like this one must have been a real test of will power.*

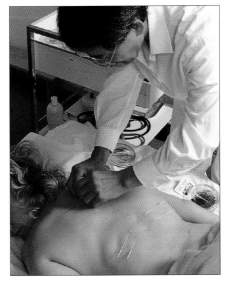

◄ *Alternative therapies such as acupuncture are said to help people give up smoking by easing the craving for a cigarette.*

smoke," sometimes up to 40-60 cigarettes a day.

Nicotine is as addictive as heroin, and as hard to give up: seven out of ten smokers have tried to quit and failed at least twice. Those who stop suddenly often feel irritable or nervous and find it difficult to concentrate, especially in the first days. The craving to give in and light up can be very strong indeed. Many people stop for years only to succumb in times of stress or in social situations. It is very hard to stay off cigarettes for good.

Those who do stop enjoy immediate physical benefits.

Twenty minutes after the last puff, blood pressure and pulse return to normal. After a day, the lungs start clearing out mucus and other smoking deposits. After two days, the body is clear of nicotine; after

three, breathing becomes easier. Within two to twelve weeks circulation improves; three to nine months later the lungs become more efficient. But it takes five to ten years to halve the risk of heart attack and lung cancer.

Giving up is possible, as millions of ex-smokers can confirm. There are many products available to help, including nicotine replacement gum, patches, or lozenges. Some people try dummy cigarettes, filters, even hypnotherapy or acupuncture. But these things help only if you are determined to succeed—the most important factor is willpower.

Whose smoke is it?

Until recently, smoking was seen as an individual choice affecting only smokers themselves. In 1988, however, a report found that those regularly exposed to secondhand cigarette smoke are 10 to 30 percent more likely to get lung cancer. Nonsmokers, who had put up with smoky bars, offices, and restaurants, now had serious cause for complaint.

▼ *Smoky air tends to be an inevitable feature of bars, but many nonsmokers find the smoke irritates their eyes, nose, and throat.*

Since then, breathing in other people's smoke, or passive smoking, has been linked with many health problems, including eye, nose, and throat irritation, allergies, bronchitis, and lung cancer.

"Breathing secondhand smoke can aggravate the condition of more than five million Americans with heart disease and 21 million Americans with chronic lung disease."
Americans for Non-Smokers' Rights

It is estimated that at least 46,000 people in the USA die every year from inhaling other people's cigarette fumes. Even pet cats and dogs have been found to suffer skin and chest complaints from their owners' smoking. The U.S. Environmental Protection Agency

◄ Most restaurants now have no-smoking areas; some have even banned smoking altogether. But smokers argue that it is their right to enjoy a cigarette with their meal.

" There is no evidence whatsoever of the dangers of passive smoking. It is merely a propaganda device to make smoking a public evil as opposed to a merely private vice. Without the passive smoking scare, there could be no argument against letting smokers kill themselves in peace. " *Bryan Appleyard, journalist*

But many experts disagree.

" The risk [from passive smoking] is small by comparison with the hazards of active smoking, but real, and it has been recognized by every independent group of scientists who examine the issue. " *Dr. Martin Jarvis, head of Cancer Research UK's health behavior unit*

(EPA) now classifies secondhand tobacco smoke as a Group A carcinogen (cancer-causing agent) for which there can be no safe level of exposure.

Only 15 percent of cigarette smoke is actually inhaled by the smoker—the rest escapes into the surrounding air. Smoke-filled rooms can have up to six times the air pollution on a busy road. Nonsmokers breathe in sidestream smoke from cigarettes lying in ashtrays, and mainstream smoke exhaled by smokers; both contain chemicals in high concentrations.

" I can't stand going into smoky bars or restaurants any more. It's horrible having to eat while people are smoking around you and it makes your eyes sting and your clothes stink. " *Jonathan, 27*

Passive smokers are now fighting back. In Australia in 2001, Marlene Sharpe, 62, of Wollongong was awarded nearly $350,000 compensation for cancer caused by working in a smoke-filled bar for 11 years. Prior to this, Meryl Roe, who worked for the Greater Manchester Council in the UK, received $40,000 compensation when passive smoking caused chest complaints that forced her out of her job.

Several countries and cities have imposed bans on smoking in public places following calls from the World Health Organization (WHO). A New York City ban on smoking in bars and restaurants went into effect in 2003, and many other cities plan to ban smoking in work places, including bars and restaurants.

► Concerns about cigarette smoke in offices have forced many employees to smoke outside.

Born to smoke?

Passive smoking is a problem for adults, but much more so for babies and children. Unborn babies are most defenseless—a mother who smokes during pregnancy carries nicotine, carbon monoxide, and other harmful chemicals in her bloodstream into that of her baby's. Nicotine makes the baby's heart beat faster, and carbon monoxide means he or she gets less oxygen.

The result can be tragic. Babies with smoking mothers are twice as likely to be born dangerously small or too early, and to suffer congenital deformities like cleft lips and palate. They are more likely to die from miscarriage, stillbirth or crib death,

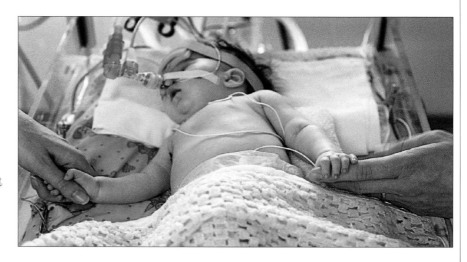

▲ *Babies born to mothers who smoked during pregnancy are more likely to be born prematurely or to have a low birth weight. Lung diseases, such as this baby has, are also more likely and there are higher instances of breathing problems.*

and suffer coughs and breathing problems during their first year. Smoking mothers are themselves at greater risk of pregnancy complications causing bleeding or their waters breaking too early.

Many women who smoke make an effort to stop while they are pregnant. Some find their body helps them.

❝ *In both pregnancies I went off smoking in the first few weeks. Even the smell of cigarette smoke made me feel sick. I knew it was bad for my baby so I was glad I didn't feel like smoking.* ❞ *Joanna Smith, mother*

Once born many babies are exposed to cigarette smoke in their homes. It is estimated that if both parents smoke an average of twenty

◀ *A woman who smokes during pregnancy subjects her baby to harmful chemicals that enter the baby's bloodstream via the placenta.*

and to be influenced by friends and siblings. In the USA, one-third of children try smoking by age 11 and two-thirds by age 16, according to 2003 records compiled by Action on Smoking and Health (ASH). The younger you start, the greater the risk of health problems later.

But many smokers believe anti-smoking groups have overreacted to the issue of passive smoking.

66 Humans have lived for 400 years suffused by secondhand smoke. Pregnant women have been smoking and adults blowing it in children's faces for centuries, and yet civilization has survived and possibly flourished. 99 Richard Klein, author and journalist

cigarettes a day, their baby will smoke the equivalent of four packs of cigarettes by the time he or she is one year old. Young children whose parents smoke have twice as many coughs and chest infections, which can cause lasting lung damage by the time they are five.

66 Environmental tobacco smoke exposure is a risk factor for new cases of asthma in children who have not previously displayed symptoms. 99 U.S. Environmental Protection Agency (EPA)

The EPA estimates that 150-300,000 American children under 18 months get pneumonia or bronchitis every year from breathing secondhand tobacco smoke, and it is well documented that children of smokers take more days off school with illness. But it may not be just their childhood that is affected.

66 There is evidence that childhood exposure to cigarette smoke increases the risk of developing cancer as an adult. 99 Americans for Non-Smokers' Rights

Children of smokers are more likely to try smoking at a young age

The giants of tobacco?

Since the first cigarette machine was invented more than a hundred years ago, tobacco manufacturers have become some of the largest and most successful companies in the world. They have a huge impact on the world economy, wielding considerable power in both Western and developing countries.

Some of the world's largest cigarette companies are based in the USA and the UK: Imperial Tobacco, American Tobacco and British American Tobacco (owner of Rothmans and Brown & Williamson in the UK, and Philip Morris and R. J. Reynolds in the USA). Tobacco company make enormous amounts of money. In the USA, tobacco-company revenues total around $50 billion every year. Many smaller countries have their own national companies producing cigarettes. China, for instance, is one of the largest producers of tobacco in the world, but smokes most of the crop itself.

Despite their success, the international tobacco companies are under increasing pressure to find new markets. As the health risks of smoking have become more widely known, the tobacco industry has fought back, first claiming that research into those risks was flawed or irrelevant, then developing low-tar brands to combat falling sales.

However, cigarette sales are still dropping in many Western countries, and new customers need to be found.

❝ The tobacco industry needs to recruit 300 new smokers a day just to replace those people killed by smoking attributable diseases. ❞
UK Health Education Authority

The major tobacco companies are now concentrating many of their resources on selling their cigarettes more widely abroad. They have already had considerable success in many of the world's developing nations, where Western cigarettes have a glamorous image.

❝ Young Chinese men in Peking and Shanghai carry Western cigarette packets with two holes: from one they offer Western cigarettes to anyone they want to impress; they use the other for their own local cheap brand to smoke themselves. ❞
Dr. Judith Mackay, director of the Asian Consultancy on Tobacco Control and adviser to health promotion agencies

Another strategy to boost profits, adopted by many tobacco companies, is diversifying into other product areas. Philip Morris, which makes Marlboro, the world's best-selling brand of cigarettes, also owns General Foods, a company whose

▲ Kenneth Clarke, former UK government minister, is now chairman of the British American Tobacco Company (BAT), which he says "maintains high ethical standards."

brands include Maxwell House coffee, Miller Light beer, and Jacobs Biscuits. British American Tobacco owns the UK finance companies Eagle Star and Allied Dunbar.

In fact, tobacco companies have such a wide presence that many people are investing their money indirectly into cigarettes without realizing it. In Australia, for example, public health professionals recently learned that $20 million of their pension funds had been invested in three tobacco companies.

Many famous brands of household products such as these are owned by tobacco companies. Philip Morris claimed that 10 percent of money spent on packaged goods in U.S. supermarkets in 1994 was on its goods.

66 *In the United States, the ten largest universities have [sold] all tobacco stock they own on ethical grounds.* **99** *Chris Rissel, Clinical Senior Lecturer, University of Sydney, Australia*

▲ *A Russian soldier smokes on a Moscow street in front of an advertisement for an American brand of cigarettes.*

Nice work if you can get it?

Producing cigarettes is a worldwide industry employing many thousands of people. In the USA, around 50,000 people work for the tobacco companies; many thousands more are employed growing tobacco in southern states like Virginia, where it is a traditional crop. Some US farming families have grown tobacco for over 200 years.

Cigarette production is also a significant source of jobs in other countries like the UK.

66 *Tobacco manufacturing brings vital economic prosperity to areas of high unemployment, such as Northern Ireland, South Wales, the East Midlands, and the North-East; the 9,500 people employed in tobacco manufacturing are among the most productive in the UK.* **99**
Tobacco Advisory Council

It is not just farmers and factory workers who benefit—sales of cigarettes also provide income for store owners, for instance. In the UK, independent tobacco sellers count on tobacco sales bringing in 25 to 40 percent of their turnover and nearly one-fifth of their profits.

▲ *A tobacco factory in Glasgow in the UK provides employment for these women in an area where jobs can be very difficult to find.*

▼ *This market selling tobacco leaves in Dubai, United Arab Emirates, is typical of tobacco markets all over the world. Tobacco can be essential to the local economy.*

▶ *Most cigarettes are sold alongside other goods, but some shops only sell tobacco products.*

❝*I have to sell a lot of things I don't agree with, like pornographic magazines, sweets loaded with sugar, and cigarettes. I can't afford to say no to all these things.* **❞**
Paul Thomas, newsdealer

However, in many Western countries jobs in the cigarette industry are becoming more scarce. In some countries, the number of people employed has dropped by three-quarters since 1979. The tobacco industry blames these losses largely on rising taxation on tobacco; their opponents say the reduction is mainly due to new technology, as more cigarettes can be produced by fewer people.

Antismoking groups argue that discouraging smoking need not lead to more unemployment.

❝*Curbing smoking would reduce jobs only very gradually and give tobacco companies time to diversify into other areas. A major study has shown that a reduction in smoking levels means that people have more money to spend in other areas like leisure, creating more work.* **❞**
Amanda Sandford, research manager, Action on Smoking and Health (ASH)

Over half of the world's tobacco is grown in developing countries like Brazil, India, Turkey, and Zimbabwe.

▶ *This tobacco farm is in Zimbabwe, which is one of the largest tobacco growing nations, along with the USA, Brazil, India, and Turkey.*

Many farmers are under contract to the large multinational tobacco companies, who offer free advice and credit for seed and fertilizer. In addition to subsidising tobacco crops, cigarette companies often set up small local subsidiaries to produce the cigarettes themselves. Labor is much cheaper in poorer countries, and there is a growing market there for cigarettes, as people are less aware of the harmful effects of smoking.

Growing and selling tobacco has definite advantages for developing countries. As well as the help from tobacco companies, they get a guaranteed price for the product. But there are problems. Tobacco is a greedy plant that quickly uses up all the nutrients in the soil and needs heavy fertilization, so land used for tobacco can become unfit for food production. Some developing countries use up to two-thirds of their agricultural land for tobacco, growing little of their own food and leaving their farmers and their governments relying heavily on the foreign tobacco giants.

Tax to stop smoking?

It is often seen as the government's role to reduce smoking through taxation and health education. Yet many governments earn money in tax whenever anyone puchases a pack of cigarettes. For example, the U.S. government earned around $15.6 billion in 2002 in taxes paid by people buying cigarettes. A significant part of the price of a pack of cigarettes is tax, which goes straight to the government, not to the tobacco company, making tobacco one of the largest sources of revenue for the government.

In comparison, governments spend only a small portion of that revenue every year on antismoking campaigns. Little will be spent on smoking education for teenagers, yet smoking groups estimate that governments receive large revenues in tax on cigarettes sold illegally to children under the age of 10.

In fact, the UK government and the European Union support European tobacco growers through an annual subsidy of almost $1.4 billion to farmers mainly in Italy, Spain, and Greece. It is hardly surprising that many people accuse Western governments of double standards, including those who actually support smokers' rights.

▼ *To avoid paying UK duty and taxes smugglers attempt to bring in tobacco products from abroad. They then sell them at "discounted" prices. The piles of tobacco products below are just a fraction of those seized in the UK by Her Majesty's Customs and Excise.*

66 *Governments who want to increase revenues, while they piously protect public health, incite more smoking by enlarging and sharpening these warnings (on the pack). This increases the pleasure for the smoker.* 99
Richard Klein, journalist and author

▶ The more cigarettes smoked, the more money governments receive in tax. Some people believe it is not in governments' interests to curb smoking and accuse them of double standards.

Some people believe there are other incentives for governments that prevent them from clamping down on smoking.

❝ *A harsh economist looking at smoking objectively would say it was a good thing. It helps people put up with lousy jobs and finishes them off just as they get to retirement age so they won't go on drawing so much old age pension.* ❞ *Emeritus Professor Michael Russell, addiction research unit*

However, tobacco companies have a great deal of political influence, putting those politicians who do oppose smoking in a vulnerable position. In the 1970s U.S. Secretary for Health Joe Califano set up a special office on smoking and health to educate the public, but tobacco farmers reacted so strongly that President Carter feared a backlash from the southern states and Califano was forced to resign.

Yet government action is vital to discourage smoking. Raising the price of cigarettes by increasing taxation is the most effective way of getting people to cut down or stop altogether—figures suggest a 10 percent price increase leads to between a 3 and 5 percent drop in consumption. But the tobacco

▼ On average the money spent on a cigarette in the USA and the UK is divided between government, retailer, advertiser, and tobacco company in these percentages.

companies are vehemently opposed to rises in taxation, arguing that it is the poor who suffer most.

❝ *It is simply unfair for the Government to expect smokers, a high proportion of whom are in the less well-off groups, to continue to be penalized for choosing to smoke, particularly when the current level of tax is so much higher than other European Community countries.* ❞ *Tobacco Advisory Council*

AVERAGE PRICE OF A CIGARETTE IN THE U.S. $ 0.13

| Advertising 11% | Tax 31% | Retailers 5% | Manufacturers 53% |

AVERAGE PRICE OF A CIGARETTE IN THE U.K. £ 0.24

| Advertising 0.8% | Tax 77.8% | Manufacturers 16.9% | Retailers 4.5% |

Promoting smoking?

Every year the tobacco industry spends huge amounts of money promoting cigarettes—around $10 billion in the UK and USA alone. Tobacco opponents say the main purpose of advertising is to encourage people to smoke by giving cigarettes a glamorous and exciting image. The tobacco industry, on the other hand, argues that the sole purpose of advertising is to persuade existing smokers to change brands; one-third of smokers change brands or buy different brands every year.

❝ *There is no convincing evidence to show that tobacco advertising encourages any individual— including children—to start smoking.* **❞** *Tobacco Manufacturers' Association*

While some countries like New Zealand, Canada, Norway, and Finland have banned tobacco advertising entirely, most countries have only restricted it—television advertisements, for instance, were banned in the US in 1970. In the past tobacco advertising in the UK was regulated by voluntary agreement— the government and the tobacco industry decided between them how and where tobacco companies could advertise. But many people felt these restrictions did not go far enough.

❝ *Virtually all the medical community believe a ban on tobacco advertising is essential. There's no evidence to show that the voluntary agreements have an impact and where there has been a total ban on cigarette adverts, it has led to a reduction in smoking.* **❞** *Amanda Sandford, research manager, ASH*

Despite the fact that cigarette advertisements were not allowed to appeal directly to young people, many worried that they encouraged children to take up smoking. They argue that tobacco promotion sends children confusing messages—how

▼ This advertisement for the UK Benson and Hedges brand is deliberately cryptic. It is not obvious what product they are selling but perhaps it also implies it is "clever" to smoke.

can smoking be unacceptable if advertisements glamorize it?

❝ *Young people know what these advertisements are about far more often than adults.* **❞** *Emeritus Professor Michael Russell, addiction research unit, King's College, London, on the brand advertisements that feature cryptic visual jokes*

In response to this pressure, advertising restrictions increased. Tobacco companies began to rely more heavily on sports sponsorship, worth over millions of dollars every year. Sponsorship has the advantage of associating cigarettes with sporting excellence and glamour, and can give longer television coverage than direct advertising. But now in Europe the situation regarding both advertising tobacco companies and

PERFECTLY SUITED? (4,2,7)

13mg TAR 1·1mg NICOTINE
SMOKING CAUSES HEART DISEASE
Health Departments' Chief Medical Officers

Sweet & Cool

PLAYER'S NAVY CUT

PLAYERS
NAVY CUT CIGARETTES
10 for 6ᵈ   20 for 11½
50 for 2/5   100 for 4/8

Marlboro
Marlboro

PEUGEOT

Marlboro

Marlboro

GOOD▸YEAR   Shell   GOOD▸YEAR
PEUGEOT
7

◀ Tobacco manufacturers have often tried to associate cigarettes with an active lifestyle. This 1923 advertisement for Player cigarettes was made when the dangers of smoking were virtually unknown. It would be unlikely to be allowed today.

▼ Formula one racing has for many years been a popular stage for tobacco advertising but in 2006 a ban on tobacco advertising at this and other worldwide sporting events will come into effect. Many people fear that finding alternative sponsors will be extremely difficult and may badly damage the sports involved.

their sports sponsorship is set to change radically.

A UK ban on tobacco advertising came into effect in 2003, and a European Union directive of December 2002 ordered a ban for all member states by July 31, 2005. This directive prevents tobacco sponsorship of international sports, such as Formula One racing and World Snooker. A UK ban on sport and cultural sponsorship within the country by tobacco companies became effective in July 2003.

66 *In relatively free market economies like Thailand, Taiwan, Singapore, Iceland, Italy, Norway, Finland, and Sweden, despite the imposition of [advertising] bans, total and per capita cigarette consumption has risen in all these countries.* 99 *Freedom Organization for the Right to Enjoy Smoking Tobacco (FOREST), UK*

Too high a price to pay?

Life for smokers can be expensive. An average U.S. smoker starting at age 20 will spend about $55,000 before retirement—the cost of a house in many areas of the country. Unfortunately, the price of smoking often hits the poorest hardest.

It is estimated that 20 percent of the UK's poorest households pay more tobacco tax than income tax, yet the government seems content to continue to ask smokers to pay out more than their fair share.
Tobacco Advisory Council on government tobacco duty

Yet it is often the poor who find it hardest to stop.

Half of the most affluent smokers have now given up but only 5 percent of the most deprived have done so. Seventy percent of the people who can least afford it still smoke.
Martin Jarvis, Cancer Research UK

Smoking can be an expensive habit, but many people are prepared to pay for the relief it brings from stress and boredom—and quitting can also be costly. For example, nicotine replacement patches, proven to increase the chances of

quittingsmoking successfully, are not cheap and a supply must be bought on a weekly basis.

Not everything, however, is more expensive for smokers. While life insurance can cost up to 40 percent more, one UK insurance company now offers smokers higher retirement incomes on some pension funds. Why? Because it knows from research and statistics that regular

smokers are likely to die sooner.

But the cost of cigarettes does not just fall on individuals. Lost working days cost U.S. employers $10 billion annually. In the UK 50 million working days a year are lost through illness related ito smoking. Smokers at work waste an average of a day a week in smoking breaks. In 2002, a spokesperson for the U.S. Centers for Disease Control said smoking-

▶ Cigarettes are probably one of this homeless man's greatest expenses. But it is far harder to kick the habit when living on the breadline.

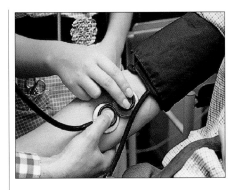

▲ *The cost of health care is huge and, with money scarce, some doctors have refused to treat people with smoking-related diseases.*

▶ *This Siberian worker's cigarette break costs his company time—and money. At ten minutes a*

related medical costs and lost productivity cost over $150 billion. Estimates of the annual cost of treating smoking-related diseases in the USA range from $24 billion to $75 billion.

Smoking also drains global resources. Modern cigarette production, for example, uses

almost four miles of paper an hour. One tree is burned in the process of curing and drying enough tobacco to be rolled into 300 cigarettes—around one tree every 14 days for the average smoker. This results in the 5-11 million acres of forest being chopped down every single year.

Many fires are started by cigarettes. The UK Home Office puts smokers' materials as the second highest cause of accidental fires in the home, causing 162 deaths and 2,100 casualties in 2000. Many forest and scrub fires are also caused by careless smokers.

◀▲ *One of the worst fires ever in the UK was at King's Cross subway station in 1987. Started by a match or cigarette, it killed 31 people and led to a smoking ban on the London Underground.*

What is being done?

Most Western countries have campaigns against smoking, usually aiming to educate people about the dangers of smoking and force governments to restrict the tobacco industry in areas like advertising.

Increasing public awareness of the health risks is a major area for anti-smoking campaigners. National no-smoking days are now common, and health warnings are compulsory on every cigarette and loose tobacco pack. The discovery of a link between passive smoking and disease has added fuel to the campaigners' fire—smoking is now banned in many public places, including public transportation, stores, restaurants, and schools.

Some individuals are tackling the tobacco industry head on. In 2000, a court in Florida upheld a compensation award of $145 billion for smoking injuries, to be paid by tobacco companies to some 700,000 people in a landmark court ruling. The three main representatives also won a total of $12.7 million.

Many private companies are now also taking action, banning smoking in the workplace or restricting it to certain areas. In 2003, one Berlin publisher had all employees sign a contract saying they would not smoke at work or anywhere else.

▲ No-smoking days are a popular and effective way of drawing the public's attention to the benefits of quitting.

NO SMOKING

◄ No-smoking signs are simple and easy to recognize. They are also becoming more common in public places.

66 *[Our employees] can't smoke in their free time, either, that would be a breach of contract. We want to send a signal to protect non-smokers.* 99 *Frank Woeckel, business manager, Eitmann-Verlag, quoted in a German newspaper*

Some smokers, however, see work restrictions as an infringement of personal liberty.

66 *Who the hell do these people think they are? If a policy to ban all smoking inside and outside buildings is allowed it would set a precedent saying that employers can stipulate the lifestyle of their employees.* 99 *Marjorie Nicholson, former spokesperson for FOREST*

The U.S. Office of Disease Prevention and Health Promotion has begun an antismoking website for kids, including a video featuring actor Bill Cosby. The U.S. Surgeon General's Report for Kids About Smoking has warnings like: "Kids who start smoking are more likely to get lower grades in school."

66 *The public may think of cigarettes as no more than blended tobacco rolled in paper, but they are more than that. Some of today's cigarettes may, in fact, qualify as high-technology delivery systems that deliver nicotine in quantities sufficient to create and to sustain addiction in the vast majority of individuals who smoke regularly.* **99**
Dr. David Kessler, former head of the FDA

Goals of Australia's National Tobacco Strategy in 2003 were to reduce: smoking; the availability and promotion of tobacco products; exposure to secondary tobacco smoke. The UK's National Health Service conducted a large drive in 2001 and 2002 to reduce smoking among the country's South Asian population, who suffer from more heart problems.

66 *'Secondhand smoke: smoking near children' is a new phase of the Department of Health's ongoing Tobacco Information Campaign. It is estimated that, in the UK today, 42 percent of children live in a house where at least one person smokes.* **99**
UK Department of Health website

But are governments simply following the mood of the times? More and more nonsmokers are now prepared to fight for their right to clean air, even if that just means approaching smokers in no-smoking zones and asking them politely to put out their cigarette.

Should smoking be banned?

Should we have the right to choose whether to smoke? Tobacco, like alcohol, was around long before anyone was aware of the risks. A ban would be difficult to enforce, as proved by the U.S. prohibition on alcohol earlier in the last century. On the other hand, many drugs like cannabis have already been classed as dangerous and made illegal.

Smokers and nonsmokers are caught in a deadlock about our freedom to smoke. Some believe no-smoking bans have gone too far. In New York, a silhouette of the former President Franklin D. Roosevelt,

▲ *Antismoking campaigners argue that addiction restricts personal liberty: a smoker is a prisoner of his or her addiction.*

▼ *Smuggled alcohol is poured down the drain in the U.S. during the Prohibition era. Banning alcohol proved impossible to enforce. Banning smoking might cause similar problems.*

which shows him smoking has been removed as it is believed it may encourage smoking. Smokers argue, like the slogan on the UK Philip Morris advert, that "the passion to regulate down to the finest detail of people's lives can lead to infringements of personal liberty."

However, those opposed to tobacco are equally steadfast.

❝ *Smokers' inability to quit despite wanting to and in the face of proven smoking-related disease is the biggest restriction of personal liberty.* ❞ *Dr. Martin Jarvis, Cancer Research UK*

As we gain more information about the risks to smokers and nonsmokers alike, campaigns to curb cigarettes are gaining momentum. Current policies appear to favor the antismokers.

❝ *Smoking is not going to go away overnight...[but] the prospects are better than they have been in 30 years.* ❞ *Scott Ballin, former chairman of the U.S. Coalition on Smoking or Health*

Many countries are adopting or tightening restrictions on advertising and promotion of cigarettes, smoking in public places, and the sale of tobacco. According to the World Health Organization, one-third of schools and places of

◀ Discarded cigarettes cause many fires every year. If smoking were banned, each country would be spared an enormous cost in terms of human life, the natural environment, and property.

package of measures to reduce smoking, including health education and support to quit, high taxes on cigarettes, a ban on advertising and promotion, more smoke-free areas, and tighter controls on underage smoking.

As long as cigarettes are so profitable, it is unlikely that they will ever be banned completely, however damning the health evidence against them. This leaves us all with a very personal choice about whether or not to smoke. Each one of us must weigh up all the facts—for and against—and make our own decision. Is smoking worth it?

entertainment are smoke-free, as are half of public places and nearly half of health care services.

Most countries restrict access to cigarettes by young people, although this is not always effective. Estimates are that U.S. children, for instance, smoke some 10 billion cigarettes a year. Some Muslim countries have banned smoking outright. However, in many countries even those strongly opposed to tobacco are reluctant to see it outlawed, believing it would drive cigarettes, like drugs, underground.

66 *We would have a black market in cigarettes that would make the current black market in cocaine and heroine look like a Sunday-school picnic.* **99** *Arnold Trebech, former director, U.S. Drug Policy Foundation*

Indeed, it is estimated that one-third of the world's cigarettes are already smuggled. In 2002, about 17 billion cigarettes were smuggled into the UK, costing the government some $5.5 billion in lost tax revenue.

Antismoking organizations like ASH suggest that instead of imposing bans we should, like Canada and New Zealand, adopt a

▼ Smuggling cigarettes is estimated to lose governments more than $19 billion a year. However, others gain: these cigarette boys earn a living by trading on the black market in Albania.

Glossary

ACUPUNCTURE: A Chinese therapy involving piercing the skin with needles at certain points in the body. It can be used to treat various illnesses and to relieve pain as well as to help with nicotine addiction.

ADDICTION: A physical or mental dependency on a habit or substance; a strong desire to repeatedly do or take something, particularly drugs.

ARSENIC: A deadly poison that has been traditionally used in murders.

BENZENE: A gas and common constituent of gasoline. It is known to cause cancer.

BLOOD PRESSURE: The pressure of the blood on the walls of the blood vessels. It is used as a common indicator of health, with prolonged high blood pressure increasing the chances of heart attacks.

BRAND: A name of a product given to it by its makers. Marlboro is a well-known brand of cigarette.

BRONCHITIS: An inflammation of the air tubes, which branch into the lungs from the windpipe.

CARBON MONOXIDE: A colorless, odorless, and very poisonous gas found in car exhaust fumes. It can kill by depriving the body of oxygen.

CENSORSHIP: The supression, usually by government, of certain literature, speech, or materials.

CHAIN SMOKING: This describes the habit of continuously smoking one cigarette after another.

CONGENITAL DEFORMITY: A handicap or physical problem present from birth.

EMPHYSEMA: A lung condition that distends the lungs and causes breathing difficulties.

FORMALDEHYDE: A poisonous chemical. It is often used in preserving biological specimens.

HYPNOTHERAPY: A therapy involving hypnosis that can be used to help with nicotine addiction.

LIFE INSURANCE: An insurance taken out by a person to give financial benefits to relatives in the event of his or her death.

MAINSTREAM SMOKE: This is the smoke breathed out by someone smoking.

NICOTINE: A powerful and highly poisonous drug. It is the main chemical responsible for the addictive quality of cigarettes.

PASSIVE SMOKING: Breathing in other people's cigarette smoke.

PNEUMONIA: A serious inflammation of the lungs that can lead to death.

PLACENTA: The organ that develops in a woman's womb during pregnancy. It supplies the baby with the food it needs for development.

SIDESTREAM SMOKE: This is the smoke given off by cigarettes when they are alight but not being actively smoked.

SPONSORSHIP: The system by which a company gives money to a sport or an event in return for displaying its name or logo so it is seen by any audience watching.

TOBACCO: The leaves of the plant *nicotiana tabacum* and the main ingredient in cigarettes. Tobacco is a natural source of nicotine.

TOBACCO DUTY: A tax imposed by governments on tobacco products as a means of raising revenue. Tobacco tax is also used as a way of discouraging smoking. Adding more tax increases the price of cigarettes, which gives people a greater incentive to stop.

Useful addresses

Action on Smoking and health (ASH)
2013 H Street N.W.
Washington, D.C. 20006
http://ash.org

Amnesty International USA
322 8th Ave.
New York, NY 10001
www.amnesty.org

Applied Research Center
3781 Broadway
Oakland, CA 94611
www.arc.org

Canadian Civil Liberties Association
Suite 200, 394 Bloor Street West
Toronto, ON M5S 1X4
www.ccla.org

Center for Human Rights Education
P.O. Box 311020
Atlanta, GA 31311
www.accessatlanta.com/community/
groups/chre/

Co-op America
1612 K Street NW, Suite 600
Washington, DC 20006
www.coopamerica.org

The Council of Canadians
502-151 Slater St.
Ottawa, Ontario, K1P 5H3
Canada
www.canadians.org

The Edmonds Institute
20319 92nd Avenue West
Edmonds, Washington 98020
www.edmonds-institute.org

INFACT
256 Hanover St.
Boston, MA 02113
www.infact.org

Facts to think about

◆ Tobacco costs the UK National Health Service over $3 billion a year for treating smoking-related diseases. The government gets ten times that amount in tax on tobacco products.

◆ Over 430,000 Americans die from smoking-related illnesses every year.

◆ About one-quarter of Americans and one-third of Europeans smoke.

◆ Greece has the highest life expectancy in Europe despite being the heaviest-smoking nation in the world.

◆ At least 200 million working days are lost to U.S. industry every year from smoking-related sick leave.

◆ In 2002 smoking giant British American Tobacco Industries made $4 billion in pretax profits from tobacco products alone.

◆ In the USA smoking-related illnesses kill over four times as many people as road and other accidents, murder, manslaughter, suicide, illegal drugs, and AIDS all put together.

◆ Every year about 500 billion cigarettes are smoked in the USA.

◆ About 9,500 British people are employed by tobacco companies.

◆ Of people in the USA who smoke, more than 70 per cent of people polled would like to quit altogether.

◆ Each year more than 17,000 children under 5 years of age are admitted to British hospitals because of exposure to high levels of secondhand smoke.

Index